Beauty in the Pain

Living Life with Chronic Pain

Written by: H.D. Bryant

Introduction

Hi,

Let me start off by welcoming you to the crappy club of chronic pain, the club nobody wanted to join. I'm so sorry you're having to deal with pain constantly; it's exhausting, not only physically but mentally as well. How do I know this? Well, I have a rare genetic disease called schwannomatosis. I know, it's a mouthful. Took me a while to be able to pronounce it properly.

Schwannomatosis is the third branch of the neurofibromatosis family—the names just keep getting better—and it causes benign tumors, called schwannomas, to grow in my nerves throughout my body. It's a very sporadic and unpredictable disease. I deal with constant electrical, sharp, shooting, searing pain that carves and stabs its way through my body wherever a tumor is, 24/7. If you've ever been electrocuted, it's a very similar feeling. Sounds fun, doesn't it? I may not know exactly what you're going through, but I can definitely relate to being in constant, severe pain. Hopefully this little book will help you find comfort, in whatever form that may be.

My Story

A brief background into my life: I went undiagnosed for eleven years. That's how rare my disease is; they didn't discover my particular gene mutation until 2011. Doctors couldn't understand why I was growing so many tumors in my left shoulder, or why I was having shooting electric pain coming and going throughout my entire body. But my journey with chronic pain really started when I was eighteen, after a motorcycle accident; being young and thinking you're invincible causes you to make ridiculous choices. We think we know everything at that age.

Long story short, I crashed the bike into an apartment complex garage and embedded the motorcycle into a wall. I wasn't wearing a helmet, my flip-flops vanished, and I woke up on the ground. I was very disoriented and had no idea how I ended up on the pavement with the bike sticking out of the wall, still running, and starting to smoke. Plus the garage door was still intact and down, though I could have sworn I was being wrapped up in metal when I hit it; at least that's what it felt like. Turned out I was able to push the garage door open—it felt like flimsy paper—because the impact of the crash completely dislocated it.

I had road rash on one side of my face and blood on my shoulder. Looked like I got into a lovely fight with the asphalt and lost. I should have gone to the hospital, but I didn't have insurance at the time and was terrified of the medical bills I would incur. So I had my friends keep an eye on me for a few days. It was so ridiculously stupid on my part to risk my health because of fear of not being able to pay a medical bill. Sad that our health system is so broken people are afraid to seek medical attention for fear of not being able to afford the care.

Over the next few months following the accident, my left shoulder was in immense pain that stopped me from lifting things and kept me up at night. That started to affect my work because I was a beverage cart girl for a golf course at the Kierland Westin Hotel in Phoenix, Arizona. When you have to wake up at

4 a.m. to serve golfers, also you're not getting sleep because the pain keeps you up, and you're not able to lift stock into your cart, that makes work pretty unbearable to say the least.

Three months after the accident I couldn't stand the pain anymore, and I finally received health insurance through work, so my doctor referred me to an orthopedic surgeon. I had an MRI scan done and the surgeon saw a cluster of masses he thought were cysts and a torn ligament. So I had my first shoulder surgery to repair the torn ligament and he also tried removing a few of the "cysts." The surgery helped in some ways but also caused more issues. I wish I had received a second opinion, but I was young and unaware of how the health-care system worked. Removing some of those "cysts" caused nerve damage, and to this day I have numbness and tingling in my shoulder, and my left arm and hand sweat more than a man. It's disgusting and very frustrating to deal with. I never let the accident or the surgery stop my pursuit of happiness though.

I guess you could say I was a restless soul and loved adventures, constantly moving from state to state. Eventually I moved to an island in the Caribbean, St. Maarten. In St. Maarten I found my passion for scuba diving. I can't explain the pure joy I felt when diving. It was simultaneously peaceful and exhilarating, and the wildlife was incredible to behold. I lived there for a year and loved the first six months, but after a while it sunk in that I was stuck on an island. I started to feel trapped and restless. I would dream about escaping, but I was caught in a toxic relationship. I was afraid to accept the truth and get the courage to leave. Then a hurricane hit and destroyed a lot of the island, and the guy I was with ended up cheating on me. I guess that was the universe's way of getting me to move on with my life.

When I came back to the States, I started working a variety of jobs at the same time, one being a receptionist at a yoga studio that shared the building with a rock-climbing gym. I'm so grateful for that job because it introduced me to my love for rock climbing; a love that I eventually introduced my husband to. I met my husband, Chris, at one of my other jobs as a swim teacher for little kids. We taught swim lessons together for a few years.

When Chris got the offer to run a swim school in Dallas, Texas, he asked if I would go with him. I of course said yes, and we moved from Phoenix and started our journey together. Chris was the general manager and I was the assistant GM, but we worked the same hours as if we had been the owners, working over sixty to seventy hours a week at that place. Eventually, lifting kids and teaching them to swim took a toll on my shoulder. The pain started to increase more and more, so I took a ton of ibuprofen, which in turn caused me to have ulcers. In case you didn't know, anti-inflammatory pain relievers cause ulcers in your stomach; not a fun side effect.

One day during swim lessons the pain was so intense that I actually passed out in the pool. Thank God Chris was there to pull me out of the water; it was a terrifying experience. One of the kids' parents worked at a hospital and recommended an orthopedic surgeon to take a look at my shoulder. The surgeon wanted to see if steroid injections would help with my pain. He thought it was just inflammation causing my issues; if only that was the case. I will never forget the pain from that steroid injection. He used a five-inch needle and moved it around in my shoulder to make sure the steroid seeped into the joint. It burned so badly and the pain from moving the needle around was agonizing. I cussed like a sailor and cried so hard afterwards. Needless to say, the injections didn't work at all.

I eventually had my second surgery. When this doctor opened me up, he didn't expect to see what he did. He had to re-attach my bicep muscles because the first surgeon had apparently (and unbeknownst to me) cut my collarbone, which basically had serrated my bicep muscle over time. This surgeon then cut more off of my collarbone because I was developing arthritis on it. He removed one of the "cysts" and sent it off to pathology. The results came back that it was a schwannoma. Unfortunately, they didn't think to get a genetic test done to see why I was developing these schwannomas, and being in my early twenties I didn't even know to ask for such a thing.

The surgeon said he had never seen so many in a shoulder before, and actually documented my case in his book. So, fun fact, I'm in a medical book somewhere! Sadly, that surgery didn't help much either. I felt as if I was getting worse. I eventually became addicted to pain pills because that was the only thing that would allow me to sleep and help numb my brain to the pain.

Chris finally told me that I wasn't eating and that he was worried about me. I had no idea I wasn't eating anymore; that's how numb the opioids made me. With his help, I quit cold turkey. Those were some of the hardest nights, coming off the pain pills. Profusely sweating all night and vomiting constantly, I felt like I was dying. I eventually pulled through and overcame the detox but my pain was still ever present, and aspirin didn't even touch it. The doctor kept changing medications to see what would help but nothing seemed to work.

Chris proposed and we married not long after. I honestly don't know how he dealt with me during those times. I was a recovered addict and in constant pain. I couldn't physically teach kids to swim anymore, so I ran the front desk and did all the paperwork for the school instead. We eventually left that place after we realized the owner wasn't ever going to sell to us and was just going to continue to dangle that golden carrot. I started as an au pair (a fancy word for nanny) for one of the families I'd taught swimming. The mom is a phenomenal woman and an accomplished bariatric surgeon, so she knew quite a few orthopedic surgeons. She introduced me to my third surgeon, who basically did a cleanup of the first two surgeries. He didn't touch the schwannomas because he didn't deal with tumors. But he used a cadaver tendon to reattach my collarbone to the shoulder and to stop the damage to my bicep muscle, which he first had to reattach.

I always joke that I'm a bit like Frankenstein's monster; I have a dead person's tendon in my shoulder. I remember waking up from that surgery and feeling like a semitruck had driven over me.

Even after that surgery I still dealt with extreme flares of shooting, searing pain on top of the constant aching. Surgeon number three recommended a neurosurgeon for my fourth shoulder surgery, who tried removing one of the schwannomas that was sitting on my clavicle. The neurosurgeon unfortunately didn't get it all and that schwannoma eventually grew back.

I continued on with my life as best as I could, but after all these surgeries I couldn't rock climb anymore because the pain was so intense. I couldn't hold onto the grips and sometimes felt like I was being electrocuted if my shoulder was in a certain position; it was like the schwannomas were being pinched. It was heartbreaking to accept I couldn't climb anymore. I felt like a failure and a weakling. I would tell myself how pathetic I was for not being able to suck up the pain. You know how it is to have those horrible thoughts and things you say to yourself? We can be our own worst enemy sometimes. Through it all, I kept doing yoga. At least I still had that.

I love yoga because it helps keep you present while strengthening your body. I became addicted to the way it made my body feel. Yoga helped keep me strong and released tension. But unfortunately, over time, even yoga started to cause me that oh-so-familiar electric pain. I couldn't accept not doing anything physical though, and I didn't want to become stagnant. So I developed a way to avoid causing myself extra pain by using the wall or a chair, but it wasn't the same. I told myself how pitiful it was that I couldn't even do simple yoga exercises anymore. Sometimes your inner voice can be so cruel.

Being a nanny was fun, but also very hard on my body. I tried my hardest not to let my pain affect my work, but it became very daunting. Some days I was so sick of being in pain that I wanted my shoulder amputated and asked Chris repeatedly to chop it off; he never obliged. I felt bad when one of the kids would accidentally hit my shoulder and it would drop me to my knees, crying. They didn't fully realize the extent of pain I was going through. No one really does unless they've gone through it themselves.

I think that's one of the most frustrating things about chronic pain—people don't fully understand what it's like to have to deal with pain constantly unless they've experienced it themselves. The mom I worked for understood to some extent because she, too, had shoulder issues. She had a torn rotator cuff and had surgery once before on it, so she sometimes understood what I was experiencing. I'm so grateful for that family. They say things happen for a reason and I fully believe that.

One day I was driving back home from the zoo with the little girl, and all of a sudden my vision tunneled down to a pinpoint and I had to pull over immediately. I tried to remain calm because I didn't want to scare the little girl, but I was terrified. I had just essentially lost my sight for a moment, on the freeway no less, and had no idea why. Luckily, my husband didn't work too far from the zoo so he came and took us back home.

I got in with an ENT doctor the following day, who sent me to get an MRI and a CAT scan of my brain, and they found a small mass in my right front temporal lobe. He referred me to a brain surgeon that wanted to do immediate surgery to remove the mass. I was twenty-five at the time and was terrified when the doctor said he had no idea what the mass was and it needed to be taken out right away. That's a frightening thought at any point in someone's life, but especially when you're twenty-five.

The woman I worked for suggested I get a second opinion and recommended a phenomenal neurosurgeon that worked in the same hospital as she did. I'm so glad I listened to her because the neurosurgeon recommended that we monitor the mass and only take it out if it grew. We watched the mass for four years with no growth. Then everything changed in 2015.

The beginning of 2015 was a rough start to a new year. One morning I couldn't move my neck without severe pain shooting down my spine. I couldn't drive or do anything else without causing that same excruciating pain. I went to my neurosurgeon and he injected steroids into my neck. To my relief it helped ease the shooting pain down my spine, but my shoulder pain worsened and sent pain up and down my arm. Then a few months after that, my father was killed in a horrible car crash. My world was turned upside down. Not only did I have to learn to cope with my father's death, but I also had to deal with new pain in my right forearm and lower back and the doctors couldn't figure out why. I felt like my life and body were falling apart.

So I get what it's like when you're first trying to figure out why you're constantly having pain that randomly comes and goes, and doctors don't have answers for you. It can be scary, frustrating, and make you start to doubt your sanity at times. I definitely felt like I was going crazy in the beginning stages of my disease. My neurosurgeon couldn't understand why I was having this electrical pain shooting down into my hand in my right arm; they did MRI scans and couldn't find anything. I even had one physical therapist massage my forearm because she said tension-building knots were causing the pain. When she hit the spot where the "invisible" tumor was, it brought me to tears. She said, "I know it hurts getting knots worked on. But it needs to be released ... just breathe through it."

I wish I had just listened to my body and made her stop; I didn't go back to her, to say the least. Then, over time, the tumor kept getting bigger until eventually you could see a bulge in my right forearm. The tumor was embedded inside the muscle nerve, which connected to the first three fingers in my dominant hand. That, in turn, made holding things extremely painful.

I used to be a painter, and creating landscapes or showcasing animals brought so much peace and joy to my life. But I started constantly dropping the paintbrush because of the pain, and it became evident I couldn't paint anymore, which was soul-crushing. Not to be able to fulfill your passion is very hard to accept and let go.

It wasn't just paintbrushes. One Thanksgiving I was trying to help and picked up a glass bowl of mashed potatoes. Right at that moment searing pain shot down into my hand and I completely lost control of holding the bowl. It shattered and sent mashed potatoes everywhere. I started crying and Chris tried to joke that if I didn't want the potatoes I could have just said so. That helped calm me down, but to lose the ability to do such simple tasks was depressing, and I would let anger get the best of me in those moments sometimes.

I eventually had to stop being a nanny because I couldn't keep up with what the job entailed. At night when I was on the couch watching a movie because the pain wouldn't allow me to sleep, I would berate myself on how worthless I was. I felt like a crazy invalid because I didn't understand what was happening to my body, and the doctors didn't have any answers. Before the tumor was big enough to detect in my forearm, I felt like I was imagining the pain, and then something or someone would bump it, and it would send the shooting pain into my hand. Almost like the tumor was saying, "Hey, don't forget I'm here!" I knew I wasn't making up what I was feeling when those moments happened; I just couldn't figure out why.

I continued to monitor the brain mass, and in 2016 I learned that it had grown. I always wonder if the trauma from losing my father, combined with the increasing physical pain, had anything to do with the growth. Studies have shown that negativity has ways of changing the body, but I guess I'll never know.

Since the mass had grown, it had to be removed. I then had to prepare for probably one of the most terrifying procedures of my life: brain surgery. I remember the days and nights leading up to that surgery. I would cry and confess to Chris how terrified I was. I was scared of dying, or becoming a completely different person, or not remember anything or anyone. Chris has always been such a rock for me, and he would assure me we had an incredible doctor who knew what he was doing, and no matter what, Chris would be there by my side. He'll never understand how much those words meant to me. To have support like that during those times was a lifesaver.

Those moments leading up to the surgery were the scariest. I had no idea what to really expect. Though I'd had four shoulder surgeries prior, brain surgery was a whole different ball game.

In the end, the five-hour surgery was a success and they were able to remove the entire tumor. But a part of me feels like when I woke up from the anesthesia, I was a different person. The old me that went under died and a new me emerged. I know that sounds a little melodramatic but I look back on the past and don't recognize the old me. The months following were difficult, to put it mildly. I ended up having seizures and was so confused about what was going on around me that I would become irritated very easily. I would argue with Chris because I didn't understand things he would ask of me and instead of saying I didn't understand, I would lash out at him and cause a fight. I would then burst into tears because I didn't understand why we were arguing in the first place.

I felt so dumb and crazy, on top of the surgery pain in my brain and ongoing pain in my body. I was so overwhelmed with pain that I didn't know what to do or how to express what I was feeling. It took time to learn how to communicate what was going on with me. Learning to deal with my chronic pain, grieving the loss of my father at the same time, and communicating to my loved ones what I was going through was a hard lesson to learn.

A few months after the brain surgery I eventually grew very frustrated with the schwannoma growing on my clavicle; the schwannoma that had been removed before and grew back. I would accidentally hit it when getting dressed or Chris would bump it by mistake and it would instantly send searing pain shooting through my neck and shoulder; kills the mood when that happens, if you know what I mean. So my brain surgeon recommended a specific doctor that dealt with removing tumors throughout one's body.

This fifth shoulder surgery was by far one of the worst because the doctor didn't listen to me or Chris about how I react to medications. He gave me pills that I specifically told him made me vomit profusely, and we ended back up in the ER to get the vomiting and pain under control. The doctor didn't get the entire schwannoma either and it grew back again. It's maddening when some doctors refuse to listen to patients.

Luckily, my neurosurgeon cared and wanted answers. He had me take a genetic test, finally, to see why I kept growing these schwannomas. Results came back and in 2016 I was diagnosed with schwannomatosis.

The doctors in Dallas didn't really have much advice for me on how to handle my case. They refused to communicate with one another, and I was essentially the middleman between all my doctors. I got so tired and frustrated that I started searching online for answers. There's not a lot of information about my disease, nor are there a lot of clinics specifically for schwannomatosis. But I found a clinic in Seattle, Washington, at UW Medical Center. Chris and I met with the team of doctors there, and I am so grateful we did. They actually communicate with one another and have a whole team set up for patients like myself. Which is such a weight lifted for the patient.

I found the best neurosurgeon, someone who has removed three of my schwannomas so far. He has been a gift from God; the surgeries he's performed have had very limited nerve damage and he has helped give me some quality of my life back. But leading up to finding the clinic in Seattle was probably the most infuriating time in my life because I didn't know where to really begin or how to deal with being diagnosed with such a rare, painful disease. Trust me, I get what it's like trying to navigate the unknown and searching for alternative answers.

There's no handbook or manuscript on how to deal with being diagnosed with a horrible, debilitating disease. There are tools that you can find but you have to go hunt them down yourself, and that can take a lot out of you, especially if you're dealing with some sort of chronic pain, or trauma. No one is the same, and everyone has their own special issues. So, when someone goes to the doctor trying to find something to help them cope with being diagnosed with a rare disease, it doesn't mean they should be put on antidepressants. But that's what happens; often there are no alternative options recommended such as meditation, hypnosis, acupuncture, etc. It's straight to a pill.

I was put on many different types of antidepressants because I was told it would help with the pain. Instead they caused adverse reactions. One in particular made me profusely vomit like in the movie *The Exorcist*, and the pain doctor said to give it seventy-two hours. Screw that! I wasn't going to vomit for seventy-two hours in hopes that this antidepressant would help my pain. The vomiting actually added to it. Needless to say, I quit that medication promptly.

Now, there are people who don't make certain chemicals in their brains and need medications to help fill in those gaps, and that's okay! But I don't think that should be the only help available. If you don't have the building blocks to cope with life's hurdles, the medications will only take you so far. Your brain is a miraculous thing, and you will start to build up a tolerance to those pills. When that happens, you'll crash back into that dark abyss. So finding helpful, healthy coping tools and techniques is crucial to living an abundant, healthy life, especially when learning to live with chronic pain.

My best advice for you during this period is to trust in yourself and what you're feeling. My goal for this book is to help you see that you're not alone and to share ways to survive and thrive with chronic pain. I know it sounds impossible that you can live a happy life with chronic pain, but you truly can. I'm living proof. In this book you will find the techniques I've learned to help myself cope and live an amazing life with chronic pain. You'll also read about how I've used these tools to climb out of mental hell.

Step 1

Mourn your past self

"In sorrow we must go, but not in despair. Behold! We are not bound for ever to the circles of the world, and beyond them is more than memory." J.R.R. Tolkien

> *Journal entry 3/10/17:*

I hate my body. I feel like an invalid. I can't even do yoga anymore, I can't even walk my dog around the damn block. I feel so crazy and ugly now. How can Chris still love me and find me attractive? I feel like my body is emaciated just like my weakling shoulder. I'm terrified on what I'm going to be like in 5 years. Will I be bound to a wheelchair and need help the rest of my pathetic life? O god, what the hell am I going to do? I can't live the rest of my life like this, in this horrendous pain. I don't know how I am going to survive this shit disease. I miss the old days when I could at least walk down a side walk and not fear someone bumping into my shoulder and causing me pain. How pathetic that I have to plan which side I'm going to walk for fear of my shoulder being bumped. I'm absolutely terrified of what the future holds. I'm struggling and don't know what to do. I'm done, just done with everything, done with this pain. Something needs to change.

Throughout your journey with pain you will have to mourn your past self a few times, until your past self is just that, the past, and it no longer controls you. I now look at my past self with loving eyes tinged with sadness sometimes, but mostly love.

Around age twenty-eight I started losing the ability to do a lot of the things I once loved like exercising, painting, and traveling. I used to be an artist, a scuba diver, rock climber, yogi, hiker, and outdoor enthusiast; I was very active, and an independent woman. Now I can't drive, and I can barely lift a heavy pot or pan. I have to do wall exercises or chair yoga because regular exercises pinch my tumors, which is excruciating. One of the hardest things I had to learn before moving forward was to let go of who I used to be, or rather, how my body used to be. It's very difficult to accept that you can no longer do things at such a young age; no one ever expects that, but sometimes life has a way of surprising you.

Before I developed this practice of mourning my past self, I was very bitter and angry. Angry at my body, and angry at the doctors for not having answers and causing me more issues by shoving pills down my throat that caused additional pain or adverse side effects. I was also angry and resentful towards God. Don't worry, I'm not going to get all biblical or religious with you. But I did blame God, and was so mad and confused about why I was being punished. I would be curled up in the fetal position, crying and shaking with pain; I would plead with God, why am I being punished? What did I do to deserve such horrendous pain? I felt like I had to have been a horrible person to have deserved such pain in my life.

Those were very dark times. In those moments, all my husband could do was just put his hand on me to let me know he was there because to hold me would cause more pain.

Some nights I was lucky to get two hours of sleep in a row. When you're at that level of exhaustion, nothing anyone says or does helps. You get so sucked into this whirlwind of pain, sleep deprivation, and exhaustion that you become a troll; no reasoning can make sense to you in those moments. For a while there I would snap at my family for nothing, or I'd cry out of frustration about not being able to sleep. I felt like I was drowning and didn't know how to come up for air. So what do you do?

For starters, don't lie in bed tossing and turning, hoping you'll fall back asleep. Get up and make some tea; try to refrain from getting on social media or your phone because that will just wake you up more. Listen to guided meditations designed for sleep. Try taking a bath and take some melatonin before bed.

When none of that works for me, I end up watching movies to help distract my brain from the pain, usually any *Harry Potter* film. But some nights back then even *Harry Potter* couldn't distract my mind, and I would get sucked into a dark, pain-riddled thought process. I would start to think of the days I lived in St. Maarten, when I would go scuba diving in the crystal blue waters of the Caribbean. That would spur further memories of the things I used to be able to do, like my artwork which I sold in an actual gallery and a line of shoes I painted for people. Or I'd think about how I miss hiking and going on adventures with my husband. Going down that path would just add fuel to the fire of resentment and bitterness, which would start a whole vicious cycle that I couldn't get out of.

You can't go down that road or you'll get stuck down that rabbit hole, and it's a dark one. That's where your darker thoughts lie, in the deep graveyard of your past self. It's good to acknowledge those memories and feelings, but it can be a dangerous path if you chose to stay down there. You become so resentful and angry at the world and yourself that even the thought of death feels like a good idea.

Being down in those depths, I became more and more depressed and would think more than once a day about dying. The pain could be so horrendous that I would plead with God to help me, or to just kill me. I would wonder, "How am I going to live the rest of my life in this amount of pain?" It was scary and seemed like a bleak future. At that point, you're really not living. Eventually I grew tired and scared of being in that constant state of mind. One day in particular set my present mindset of grieving my past self into motion.

I was at home, and the pain was having its way with me. It was sending electrical currents throughout my body and all I could do was ride the horrible wave. After the shocks settled down I had a moment where I thought, "If I had a gun right now, I'd shoot myself." It was probably the scariest thought I've ever had. We don't own a gun and I'm grateful we don't because I know I would have used it then. I never want my loved ones to go through that, but the pain was unbearable and there seemed to be no light at the end of the tunnel.

After having that thought, I knew I had to figure something out because the road I was headed down wasn't pretty. I had to be completely honest with Chris about what I was feeling and going through. That's a hard conversation to have with your spouse, that you would have shot yourself if you owned a gun. So, I ended up taking it one day at a time, and I started to mourn my past self.

If you've never had someone die in your life that you've had to mourn, this task may be a bit difficult at first, but you can totally do it. Honestly, think of your past self as dead because, in all reality, that person is. Chronic pain changes who you are; I know I'm a completely different person than when I started this journey. No one is the same person they used to be, not even the healthiest of people. So try to start your thinking there, knowing that we all evolve over time. Then acknowledge that those things you used to be able to do are just things you're learning to let go of, and appreciate them differently.

Just because I can't rock climb right now doesn't mean I've stopped enjoying the sport. I love watching professional climbers, and live vicariously through them. You don't have to stop loving the things you used to do, you just have to appreciate them in a different way. I know how frustrating and heartbreaking it is at first, and that's why you have to mourn your past self. If you don't learn to let go of the past, it will consume you.

So how do you mourn yourself when you're still alive? Make time for yourself each day. It can be in the bath or outside watching birds; doesn't matter, but make the time to care for yourself. Look at each thing you can no longer do, and acknowledge that you loved doing that. Acknowledge that you miss it; let the tears fall. Feel the grief, but don't get too consumed by it because it can suck you in, and that's a dangerous black hole. Give yourself a time limit on how long you can cry. I know that may sound silly, but it's a great technique if you tend to be easily overwhelmed by grief.

Acknowledge the emotions, let them express themselves the way the emotions need to be, and then start to look at the positive things in your life. Yes, I can't scuba dive, but I live in a beautiful place surrounded by trees and have a loving support system. What also helps with this process is finding things you can do that bring you joy. I no longer paint, but I've started writing and creating videos on YouTube to help my creative mind, and I love it. I never thought I would become a writer, let alone post videos on YouTube. Learning to let go of your past life isn't easy, but finding new activities and hobbies helps bring joy and light to your life. I've realized I don't need to be fated to my disease, and you don't have to be sentenced to your pain. Yes, we may have our illnesses for the rest of our lives, but they don't have to dictate our happiness. You have the power to control your mind and what brings you joy and happiness. Don't give that power over to the pain which has already taken quite a bit from you.

This process is essentially grieving, and there's no timeline when it comes to grief. It's sporadic and will hit you at the most inopportune moments. When I was in the grocery store with my husband, I was hit by the fact that I wasn't able to drive anymore and I couldn't help but let the tears fall. I know it feels embarrassing when that occurs but there's nothing to be ashamed of. We all go through it at some point in our lives. Sometimes that just happens, and there's no controlling grief. So be kind and patient with yourself.

What also has helped me through this process is living in the present moment. Which brings me to my next point.

Step 2

Learn to live in the present
"Nature does not hurry, yet everything is accomplished." - Lao Tzu

Journal entry 10/30/16:

It's 1:56 am and I've been trying to sleep since 10:30. I'm watching the Goonies and texting sis because she can't sleep either due to her pain. I'm currently wrapped up in my heating pad on the couch. I'm afraid of the future....will I ever be able to travel or even leave this damn house? I never use to be afraid for what the future may look like but now every-thing has changed so drastically in such a short amount of time that I fear I'm stuck to this house, to this couch forever, wrapped up in a heating pad. O god I hate my life now....I hate my body.

I had to learn to live in the present moment because when I looked into the future, it scared me. That, in turn, caused me to have panic and anxiety attacks, which only amplified the pain. It's hard to stay in the moment when the pain is excruciating, and all you want to do is be anywhere but in your own body. Thinking of the future in those moments is a terrible idea. All I could think was that if I currently couldn't do simple tasks like the dishes or cooking, what would my future look like? I was terrified at what I would look like, what I wouldn't be able to do, and was crippled by the fear of completely losing my freedom.

I had to work on not focusing too far ahead.

So work on staying in the moment. Now, I'm not saying you'll never be able to plan, or be excited for the future. If you follow these steps you can start to be excited for what the future may hold, but you first have to work on yourself, and learn how to live with pain— while not letting it dictate your life.

I used to lash out at my loved ones. It was easier to let the pain leach out onto them than to face it myself. My husband got the brunt of it and that's no way to have a relationship with some-one. I was on this medication called Lyrica and it caused me to be super irritable. Chris left a cup over at our neighbor's house one day and I completely lost it and started yelling at him. During my outburst I realized I was upset over a freaking cup. So of course, I started to cry because I felt like I was losing control over my emotions and my life.

Now I tell the people in my life what I'm experiencing, and about the different levels of pain. I express what I need, whether that be space to take care of myself, or help to distract me from the pain. I've learned to communicate what I'm going through, and it has helped my relationships drastically.

In those excruciatingly painful moments, acknowledge the pain. If you don't, it will definitely make itself known to you in unhealthy ways. Say, "I see you, but I don't need you blinding my sight." Once you've acknowledged the pain, do something in the moment that brings you joy. That might be listening to music, taking a bath, calling a friend, or watching a movie. Whatever it is, just do it.

We've been taught throughout our lives that we always have to do something that is productive for society. That was a hard stigma for me to get over. I had always worked, including holding three jobs at the same time at one point in my life. To go from working full-time to not being able to leave the house was very hard to accept. I had to learn that it's okay that I can't work like the rest of society. That doesn't make me less of a human.

I would feel guilty for being in pain, which is something I have zero control over. I found that beating myself up over it added to the intensity. I had to give myself permission to be in pain. By accepting that it's okay to be in pain and allowing myself to feel whatever my body is going through has helped my mentality immensely.

Instead of berating myself, I began to focus on the present moment and things that bring me joy. I really started to work on this when we moved just outside of Seattle a few years ago because I was forced to be alone the majority of the time. Not being able to leave the house or even the bed sometimes was very hard to accept. In those moments I would start to think of the what-ifs, which is a treacherous path. To think of the past, or to fret about the future doesn't help the pain.

Practicing meditation is a great tool to help you remain in the present moment; it helps teach you breathing techniques, which help reduce stress and anxiety. There are audiobooks and YouTube videos that help guide you into a mindful state and help you develop a practice of staying in the moment. When you're busy thinking of the past or the future, you're missing out on what's happening now. If right now you're experiencing pain, be in it, and find ways that help you through the dark moments.

Like I said earlier, when I'm in severe moments of pain I watch movies, especially *The Hobbit* or any *Harry Potter* film. Audio books from Audible have been a great help as well; author Laurell K. Hamilton has helped distract my mind with her incredible imagination. Think of this as an opportunity to catch up on shows, books, or movies you've been dying to pick up. There's always a silver lining to things. You've just got to retrain your mind to find those positive underlying solutions.

What also helps keep me in the present is to avoid being idle. As I said before, I'm no longer able to do the activities I once loved, so I've found other ways to keep my body moving. Besides wall and chair yoga, when summer rolls around I go to the lake and just slowly wade around. When the pain isn't too bad, getting out to walk on an easy path in the woods helps my mentality drastically. Being surrounded by nature is a great reminder to stay in the present. Sometimes all I could do was sit on my porch and watch the wildlife around me.

It took a lot of practice to learn to accept my current state, and to allow myself to enjoy the simple things in my life while being in pain. So be patient with yourself and your progress. Also, developing a practice of being grateful for the things in my life has helped me stay in the moment.

Step 3

Develop a daily practice of being grateful
"The longer you linger in gratitude, the more you draw your new life to you. For gratitude is the ultimate state of receivership." – Dr. Joe Dispenza

Journal entry 11/13/17:

My life has changed so drastically in the last 2 years. I lost my dad due to a terrible car crash. My body started to deteriorate and was diagnosed with a rare and shitty fucking disease. I had brain surgery to remove a grade 2 tumor. But there's also been amazing change too. We moved to a small town outside of Seattle, WA, called Granite Falls and it's such a beautiful place to be. I have an awesome team of doctors at UW that know about my disease and trying all different kinds of meds and techniques to help my pain and to live a happy life. As I sit outside with trees surrounding me and birds singing in almost every tree, I can honestly say I love my life. It's a weird dichotomy of emotions, right? I'm in so much pain I sometimes pray to die but I don't want to die because this life I'm living is extraordinary. I have the most loving, wonderful husband. I was blessed to marry my best friend. We have embarked on so many adventures together. I know his life has been changed too but there's no one else I'd want to navigate this life with than him. This summer I found a love for kayaking and Chris would tote me around so I could enjoy it. Who does that? He's so amazing.

When my husband and I first moved just outside of Seattle, I had to develop a morning ritual to help keep me positive. Going from working and being physically active to not being able to leave the house became very burdensome and depressing. So I started a different type of morning ritual. Now, I wake up, listen to my morning meditation, do some gentle yoga stretches in bed to help wake my stiff body, take a bath to help ease the pain, make tea, take my medication, and sit out on my front porch while watching the birds feed.

During this time on the porch, I thank God for all the blessings in my life. If you don't believe in a god, you can still express gratitude for everything that is present in your life. Writing in a journal is a great way to start your gratitude practice, or you can express it in your mind, or say it out loud. At first, this practice frustrated the hell out of me because I would harp on the things I no longer had. I had to remind myself to stay in the present moment, and what I was grateful for right then and there. I was surrounded by forests and birds, which is a beautiful, melodic scene. So I started there, being grateful for the lush forest and wildlife. Then I continued to find the little things that I had around me in my life that brought me joy; family, friends, dogs, nature, movies, tea. You have to learn to celebrate the small and simple things.

We are so blessed in this life, but we sometimes overcomplicate it, and force an unrealistic image upon ourselves that tends to cripple us. Just because you're not living in a mansion doesn't mean you don't have blessings. We need to stop comparing ourselves with others. We all experience this life on our own individual paths. No one feels or deals with life and pain the same way. Stop comparing your situation to another's because it will only continue to perpetuate the despair.

I started listening to a book on Audible that really changed my views on life. Wayne W. Dyer's *Manifest Your Destiny,* changed my life for the better. Through Dr. Dyer's teachings I learned that I am in control of my life. Just because I have schwannomatosis doesn't mean my life is over; I am the creator of my own story. Dr. Dyer was the first person to introduce me to the idea of manifestation. I eventually started to implement his morning and evening

meditations every day. The evening meditation focuses on gratitude; and I have learned that I have so much to be grateful for and
no longer struggle to find things to thank God about. I cannot recommend Dr. Dyer's writings enough.

A 2009 National Institutes of Health study showed that acts
of kindness and feelings of gratitude activate a region in the brain,
the hypothalamus. The hypothalamus is the part of our brain
that regulates a number of our bodily functions including our
appetites, sleep, temperature, metabolism, and growth; it also
has a huge influence on our stress levels. When the hypothalamus
is activated, our brains are flooded with dopamine. Dopamine
feels good, which is why it's generally considered the "reward"
neurotransmitter. When we're grateful for something, our brains
reward us by giving us a natural high, and we then want to keep
doing the same thing.

I can't say it enough: your brain is a powerful tool. I definitely
feel a difference since I've started my daily practice of gratitude.
It's amazing how such a simple practice can change the way one
perceives life.

Step 4

Work on your mental state.

"The difference between a flower and a weed is judgment." - From a tea bag tag

Journal Entry 6/1/18:

I'm finding myself getting more jealous of people. Especially when they celebrate that they're getting great sleep. I need to be more cognizant of that and try to not become bitter but it's hard when your life has been turned upside down and you're not getting sleep and you're in constant pain. Then you have someone pumped that they feel great. I can't hate on them because I can only imagine what I would be like lol. I'd be obnoxious!

∞∞∞

Make sure your mentality is healthy because if it's not, you're going to have myriad of issues that follow suit, all easily preventable if you focus on your mental state. Our brain is powerful and can help break us free—or it can keep us in despair; I had to learn that the hard way. I suffered from depression and anxiety and thought about death and dying daily. I didn't want to kill myself, because I've lost friends to suicide. I know the other side of that ugly sword, and I would never put my loved ones through that, but I understand wanting peace and a reprieve from the gnawing, incessant pain.

I've been in and out of therapy since I was thirteen. You could say I was a rebel, or juvenile delinquent, whichever you prefer. I started drinking and doing drugs at that age, which spurred my lying, stealing, and running away a few times. At one point, I stole my mom's car to escape Phoenix. My parents eventually sent me away when I was fourteen to a wilderness program, then to a therapeutic boarding school where they shoved "therapy" down our throats, but that's a different story for another time.

Needless to say, I'm well-versed in therapy. I have found all different types of therapists throughout my adult life, and I am a huge advocate for people going to see someone. If you've never been to a therapist, I highly recommend finding one. It's incredible how having an impartial person to talk to helps you work through your issues and see things from a different perspective. Eventually I had to develop my own type of therapy; meditations and hypnosis have helped me through my disease, and taught me how to cope with chronic pain. I had an almost nonexistent meditation practice before my disease fully kicked in. I wish I had dived more into the shivasana part of the yoga classes I once attended. Shivasana is the meditation at the end of each class.

There are many books and websites out there designed to help you develop your personal meditation practice. You should check out www.healthjourneys.com. They have a plethora of guided audios for a variety of subjects; I especially like their guided sleep meditations. I use the surgery set whenever I have to get one of my tumors removed. It has helped me through the fear of the surgery to the healing process, and with dealing with the pain afterwards.

I'm now able to detach myself from my pain and observe it as an outsider, thanks to the multiple guided audios I've listened to. You have to find a balance between not paying too much attention to your pain—because when you do that, it can be overwhelming and amplify it, or cause more anxiety, which causes more pain—but still acknowledging the pain, because if you don't, it's like a child that will make itself known and heard. So it's a fine dance you have to learn. It's up to you to work on your state of mind, to work through chronic pain, and learn to live a happy, fulfilled, abundant life.

I highly recommended visiting www.mindvalley.com. They have wonderful articles, videos, and classes you can take online that will help build your meditation practice and help your mentality. One class in particular is the 6 Phase Meditation. It's free, and simple to implement into your daily routine. They have amazing teachers, from all walks of life, trying to help others succeed and make this world a better place. One of those teachers is Marisa Peer. I am so grateful I enrolled in her program because she helped me realize I have the power to create my dream life, taught me how to successfully break old patterns, and show me I don't need to fall victim to societal norms.

I also signed up to multiple online pain support groups, and found that some of those people just want to complain. I understand wanting to vent about what you're feeling and going through, but there's a difference between healthy venting and when it just becomes toxic. It's hard to offer advice or support when all a person wants to do is harp on all the bad that is happening in their life. So don't fall victim to those types of people; they don't help the pain. I located a support group specifically for my disease, and found a deeper connection with them. I didn't feel so alone or crazy in what I was experiencing when I connected with others who understood. Seek out others with the same ailment/disease; they will become your brethren in arms.

Another resource that has helped me is the book, *Becoming Supernatural* by Dr. Joe Dispenza. It really helped show me how much our environments have a huge impact on our health and mentality. It also taught me that I have the choice to be miserable, or I can live a happy life. Choose to live your life in happiness. You have the choice and the power to do so.

Step 5

Practice positivity
"Plant kindness, and gather love." -Proverb

Journal entry 7/13/17:

This pain is unbearable and excruciating at times. Sometimes I wish for anything to make the pain go away. But I try to think of positive things instead of how awful my situation is and tell myself there will be a cure one day and I will survive this disease.

∞∞∞

Positive thoughts really do go a long way. There's evidence that thinking positive thoughts can rewire your brain. Negativity is so contagious. Have you ever been in a great mood, then you talk to someone who sees the bad in everything? Even sunshine can be turned into a negative thing, "It's so hot out. The sun just burns me and everything to a crisp. I just hate the sun." That kind of attitude is exhausting and can make you feel anxious and drained.

When you change your words, the whole meaning and content changes. If you can appreciate things as they are, life becomes very simple. The sun helps grow our food and helps produce vitamin D, which keeps us happy and healthy. Plus you can swim more when it's sunny and hot. You can choose to live life looking through a dark lens, or you can see the beauty that surrounds you, and choose to see life a different way. It's your choice if you want to live a happy life with pain. I know that sounds crazy, but you *can* live a happy life in pain, you just have to find the beauty in it. It took me a while to adopt this mindset of finding beauty in the pain.

I get that it's hard to think positive when electric pain is wracking through your body. You can't sleep, and you're missing out on events with friends and family because of it. I know what it's like to have to sit at home on the couch or in bed with my heating pad and ice pack because the pain had a mind of its own, and I couldn't leave. In those awful moments, I watch something that brings me joy—movies, or Netflix shows have been a lifesaver. Find the things that bring light, laughter, and joy to your world. Search for the positive things in life. A positive attitude cultivates love, and we need more love in this world.

Imagine you're lying on the couch watching a funny show with your love. You both are laughing and enjoying the moment. Then, all of the sudden a searing pain stabs its way through your shoulder, up into the neck, straight to your brain. If you've ever electrocuted yourself, it's a pretty similar feeling. Well, imagine that happening at random moments, every day, without warning. You have to acknowledge the pain, but you can't focus on it or then your mind starts to feel it more and more. The process of trying not to focus on it, while still being mindful of the pain, can become draining emotionally, not to mention physically. This is my constant state of mind: mindful of the pain but trying to live in the moment, while remaining positive for my own sanity. That's why I love watching or listening to my favorite movies or comedies. I've found comedy helps distract me from the pain and is an amazing cure for many ailments. Laughter is great medicine.

Another way I help remind myself to remain positive is writing notes in my phone of thoughts or sayings that pop into my head, or something I have read or experienced, and going back later to read them. They're like little gems to find, sometimes very silly, sometimes serious, and other times profound and deep. I enjoy reading them as a reminder to stay positive. I'm my own personal coach, through Notes on my phone; sounds ridiculous, I know, but it helps.

Find ways to remind yourself of the beauty and joy in your life. I recently started writing messages on Post-it notes and placing them on my mirror. That way I see them all day, every day. I choose positivity over misery because I will be in pain either way; I'd much rather be happy and in pain than miserable and in pain.

I also try to be kind to everyone I meet or speak with. Odds are they have their own demons they're fighting. Remember to be kind and understanding, not only to yourself, but others as well. You really don't know what another person is going through. So don't take it personally if they lash out at you or ignore you; it's not you, it's them.

Step 6

Practice not taking what people say or do personally

"Loving yourself changes the way you love others." -Frida Kahlo

Journal Entry 7/4/17:

Our neighbors invited us over for a BBQ today. We went for a little while because I needed to get out of the house and see some people. I hate how this disease has made me cooped up in the house. But at least it's beautiful outside and a perfect day for a BBQ with the neighbors. They had a few of their friends over so it was nice to meet new people but this one woman made me feel really insecure about myself. She basically said I look fine and doesn't look like anything is wrong with me. She had asked what do I do.

There are times when I meet new people and they'll ask what I do for a living and I use to experiment with different responses, now I just tell them the truth but I would feel a sort of shame from not being able to work. On the outside, I look like a normal woman. My pain and disease lies deep within my body. I didn't want to tell people I couldn't work, and feel their judgmental eyes scanning me for a good reason why I can't contribute to society like a normal person. Sometimes I would tell people I'm currently looking, even though I couldn't. It was easier to deal with a response from that than from, "I don't work because I have a disease that debilitates me from working." After a while I decided it's not worth the energy to lie about something I don't have control over. I've accepted my reality, to some extent. I still have moments of guilt, anger, you know all the lovely accoutrement. Now some people become curious about my disease and ask me questions. While others just dismiss me as a moocher, or honestly don't care what my response is. But like I said, it's been a journey of self-reflection. I'm trying to not let other's judgments affect me, but I am human. This disease has definitely made me less judgmental myself though. It's taught me humility and my compassion for others has grown immensely. It's definitely hard to not take what she said personally though. But I need to remember I can't control my pain, I can control my emotions and how I respond to people like her.

∞∞∞

This step has been a work in progress for sure. I'm a very sensitive person by nature, and I had to learn to build barriers to protect myself. Barriers were helpful when I was younger and living in a toxic environment, not able or aware of how to cope with trauma. As an adult, those types of mental blocks are not helpful or beneficial; they start to cause more issues in your life, especially in your relationships. To start tearing down those walls, I had to develop coping techniques, one being not taking everything personally. I have to remember that I can't control what others will say, think, or do, but I can control how I react to them.

This lesson has been a difficult one to learn. I mentally and emotionally concur with the idea, but with the walls gone, my emotions are open to the world and it's scary. I've got to remember that I can live with my heart on my sleeve and be genuine without the hurt, as long as I don't take things personally. I've gotten really good with strangers, friends, and some family. But I still have a hard time with the ones closest to me; those hurts can be the deepest, and I have some old scars.

I'm getting better every day because I've made that mental choice that I will no longer live this life closed off, or run by other's emotions and actions. I have taken back control of my life by taking control of my emotions, and learning not to take things personally has been a huge factor. It has helped drastically in my medical career. Just because I didn't go six years or more to college to become a doctor, or have an exponential amount of student loan debt, doesn't mean I didn't go the back way in. I have fourteen years of being a chronic disease/pain patient, and I have an exorbitant number of medical bills that have been sent to collections; perspective. I'm not saying I operate on people or save people's lives. Just that the medical field has multiple careers, and one is being the patient.

Not taking things personally has helped me deal with egotistical doctors who are unwilling to admit they are wrong or don't know what is going on. To bitchy nurses who are overworked or maybe just had a patient die. Learning to detach from other's emotions and reactions has been a lifesaver. You never know what other people are going through or what's going on in their head. Just like they don't understand what you're going through. We may share our lives with others, but we're still alone on our own journeys. Remembering this has helped me not take someone's anger personally.

Sometimes life can just pile it on, and a person can only take so much before they snap. That is by no means a reflection on me. I know I don't treat others like that, so I know that's not me and that person doesn't reflect who I am. Be patient and kind not only with yourself but with other people as well. This process isn't easy, but it is doable.

Hey, you may find this to be the easiest one to learn, and if so, my hat is off to you. Keep shining and living your life! But if you're like me, it's okay. There are great books out there, one being *The Four Agreements* by Don Miguel Ruiz. That book really helped me with this particular lesson. I've read it multiple times throughout my life, and it has helped each time. One of the Post-it notes I wrote and stuck on my mirror says, "Don't take anything personally." It's a very helpful reminder when starting off your day while brushing your teeth.

Step 7

Keep a journal

"Journal writing is a voyage to the interior." – Christina Baldwin

Journal Entry 7/19/18:

I'm in the hospital dreading that I've got a tumor growing deep inside my stomach. I was hoping and wishing it was my appendix instead of growing a tumor. How sad that is where you wish for a different medical issue because you know what that means if you're growing a tumor.

∞∞∞

At the beginning of my disease, my pain fluctuated drastically, and it was hard to explain to doctors what I was experiencing. I started a pain journal documenting what activities triggered my pain and what level it would reach. Eventually the pain became constant, and nothing and everything triggered it. So, keeping a pain journal became pointless, but in the beginning it was helpful to show the doctors what I was going through.

When dealing with doctors I found writing out my questions in advance helped me drastically. I'm sure you've been there when you have all these questions but all of a sudden can't remember any of them at the time of your appointment. Write out your questions and concerns; I got a little journal solely for this purpose. Bring the medical journal to the appointments and write everything down. Don't be afraid to ask questions; this is your life and your body. You have every right to know what's going on and what your options are. If you don't get an answer, go home and research the crap out of it, or get a second opinion.

I've found having a medical journal is very helpful after surgeries, especially after my brain surgery. You're so doped up on heavy medications that you tend to forget things. So it's helpful to have the doctors' responses written down. That way if you forget what was said, you can look back at your journal.

Keeping a regular journal is very helpful too. When you bottle up emotions, that's when you start to develop health issues. Your body will express what you are feeling and experiencing in many different ways from headaches to ulcers to anxiety, and anything in between. At my therapeutic boarding school we were asked to keep a daily journal. At first, I fought this because I hated expressing my emotions, and didn't want to face them head-on. The journal laid them flat out in front of me. Over time this practice helped me immensely, and later on in life helped me with my pain journal. Don't be ashamed of what you are feeling, thinking, and going through.

When I was attending boarding school, my best friend from Phoenix died. My school wouldn't allow me to leave and go to her funeral. I was fifteen at the time and had no idea how to cope with such a death. My school wasn't much of a help either, which is ironic for being a "therapeutic" boarding school. So I found my own way to cope; I started a journal dedicated to her. I would write to her every day and purge whatever I was feeling or going through. I still have that journal to this day. Over time I began to accept that she was gone, but I didn't have to forget about her. That journal gave me an outlet to say my goodbyes and apologize for dragging her into the drug world and not being the friend she deserved. It also helped me forgive myself.

You can have a journal for different situations throughout your life. It's a healthy way to accept your reality and express whatever emotions or thoughts you're having without feeling judged.

Step 8

Don't stop searching for answers

"If you want to awaken all of humanity, then awaken all of yourself, if you want to eliminate the suffering in the world, then eliminate all that is dark and negative in yourself. Truly, the greatest gift you have to give is that of your own self transformation." - Lao Tzu

Journal Entry 12/9/17:

Pain doctor has essentially ran out of options for me. We're now doing lidocaine IV infusions to see if it will help dull the nerve endings. Being hooked up to an IV for an hour waiting to see if this will help decrease the pain has become exhausting. When I'm hooked up to the IV my pain is brought down to a 4 which feels like such a reprieve from my normal 7-10's, that it almost feels like a 0 but I still feel the pain...if that makes any sense. This disease makes me feel crazy sometimes, especially when trying to explain this to the doctor. But once the medicine is done my pain goes up to a 6 and will fluctuate between a 6 and 8 for a few days then I'm back up to my "normal" pain levels reaching 10. I'm so sick of this pain and the pain doc not knowing what else to do for me. At least he's on board with the medical marijuana.

When you have doctors saying they don't know what else they can do for you, or they start to experiment on you and nothing is working, you have every right to search for alternative solutions, and that's exactly what I did. I was sick of the pain-ridden life, and not being able to experience things anymore. So I started researching alternative solutions around the world.

After the prescriptions from the doctors failed, I started to look towards the cannabis route. During my research into cannabis I found so many successful stories from patients suffering from a variety of ailments like seizures, chronic pain, and so much more. I spoke with my neurooncologist and she was all for me trying medical marijuana. After I received my medical card, I went to different dispensaries and was overwhelmed by the variety of products. I'm lucky enough to live in a state where cannabis is legal, and here in the state of Washington cannabis is not only medical but recreational as well.

It took a lot of experimenting with different products to finally find the combination I need. I eventually found that a 50:50 ratio, meaning I need equal amounts of CBD and THC in a product, works best for me. I currently use a tincture that is equal parts CBD and THC, a rub for my spasming muscles, and a vape pen. CBD and THC function better together as they work off one another, which is called the entourage effect. CBD not only helps with my seizures but also eases my anxiety and depression.

When the seizure medications failed, my husband couldn't stand to watch me go through the seizures anymore. So, we got a CBD vape pen and used it while I was suffering from a seizure. It instantaneously worked and my body stopped seizing out; it's been three years since that day, and I haven't had a seizure since, thanks to CBD. My story is not the only one like this. I highly recommend looking up Sanjay Gupta's documentary, *Weed*, which is about marijuana and its effects. In the documentary you're introduced to a little girl named Charlotte who suffered from three hundred seizures a week. CBD cut that to two to three seizures a month. It's incredible what this medication can do.

Unfortunately, CBD didn't stop my severe pain, so I added THC to the mix. It helps with my arthritis, sleep, nausea, and increases my appetite; when the pain is so bad, you're not hungry and feel super nauseous. So to finally get a little bit of respite from some of those issues was a blessing. But cannabis isn't a cure-all, unfortunately. I still suffered tremendous nerve pain. As I continued searching for answers, I found kratom.

Kratom is a tree that naturally grows in Thailand, and has a long and tempestuous history. The Thai government made kratom illegal when it started to infringe upon the profitable opium market. The Thai government passed a series of laws that levied duties and taxes on every aspect of the opium trade from the growers to the manufacturers, distributors, shop owners, and consumers. But with a boom in opium consumption, there was also a boom in opium addictions, opium-related deaths, and general public health concerns; much like the opioid epidemic we're having now in the United States.

In the 1930s, the people of Thailand discovered that kratom leaves were a powerful means of helping them with their opium addiction. Not only did kratom trees grow everywhere in Thailand, but kratom was free, safe, non-addicting, and natural. Many new opium addicts used kratom to alleviate their symptoms. Workers in the fields found that not only did kratom help alleviate the pain they felt from all of the hard physical labor, but it provided them with a mild sense of calm, and helped them get through their labor-intensive days.

The Thai government eventually started to feel the repercussions from people switching from opium to kratom. In a special meeting on January 7, 1943, a member of the House of Representatives from Lampang, Police Major General Pin Amornwisaisoradej, said, "Taxes for opium are high while kratom is currently not being taxed. With the increase of those taxes, people are starting to use kratom instead and this has had a visible impact on our government's income." So in 1979, kratom was included in the Thai Narcotics Act, under Schedule 5. It was added to the same classification that cannabis and psilocybin mushrooms belong to and imposed severe penalties for ingesting kratom.

Based upon this information, you may be asking where can you get kratom. Well, Indonesia doesn't feel the same way as the Thai government, and the country grows and exports kratom. We have kratom suppliers all over the USA who mainly get their kratom from Indonesia. I heard about kratom from a podcast and it piqued my interest. I continued to look further into the plant and watched a documentary on Netflix called a *Leaf of Faith*, which was mentioned in the podcast. Some retired athletes spoke about how kratom has saved their lives, and I started to cry with these athletes because I could relate to what they were talking about. They had doctors shoving opioids down their throats and were still in severe pain, plus suffering from the plethora of issues that accompany opioid use. So, I found a reputable store online that sold kratom and ordered some.

I first tried kratom in powder form but couldn't stand the taste. It was just way too bitter, and downright disgusting to me; a mix between a wheat- grass shot and crushed-up pills. But luckily this supplier had kratom capsules, and I gave them a go. I was blown away by how much kratom helped my nerve pain. I hadn't experienced relief like that ever. It didn't completely take away the pain but it got me to a consistent level six, even a five sometimes, instead of a fluctuation to ten.

Schwannomatosis is so sporadic and unpredictable which makes treating the pain difficult. Combining kratom and cannabis when I'm at a level ten has helped exponentially. With the blessing of getting some relief, I continued to search for answers that could continue to improve my quality of life.

Just because the United States doesn't have the answers for me doesn't mean they can't be found somewhere else. There are quite a lot of different choices out there, from shamans to different types of blood transfusions, and everything in between. It took a lot of time and patience to find reliable information. Our government has skewed views on health care, which makes researching alternative treatments very difficult.

During months of research, and phone conversations with professionals in varying fields, I found a solution: stem cell therapy. I won't bore you with all the scientific jargon, but embryonic stem cells are efficient at repairing damaged cells, nerves, and so much more. They are our building blocks when we're first developing in the womb. When people hear 'embryonic stem cells,' they automatically assume these cells are harvested from dead babies, and this could be further from reality. When stem cells are harvested from embryonic fluid, neither the mother nor the baby is injured in this process.

If you have ever had a baby, you have probably had the test where they extract embryonic fluid to test for diseases and precursors. Well, they used to throw out that fluid once it was tested. Now, they save that fluid and extract stem cells from it. They're also extracting it from umbilical cords, and advising parents to save their baby's umbilical cords for future emergencies. There are decades of research for stem cell treatments, with countless documented successful cases.

Israel is making great strides in the medical field, especially in stem cell therapy. People with Parkinson's disease and multiple sclerosis are seeing incredible results from receiving stem cell treatments. So, my thought process was, these are neurological issues, and my disease is neurological; if they're seeing great results, then it will definitely help me. Unfortunately, Israel wanted over $30,000, and I couldn't afford that type of treatment. So, I continued my search and came across a facility in Panama. This specific facility treated Mel Gibson's father and saved his life. There's a great podcast by Joe Rogan where he interviews the doctor and Mel Gibson. You should definitely check it out.

Unfortunately, the Panama facility won't accept me until I'm in my forties. So I kept on searching, like Dory says in *Finding Nemo*, "Just keep swimming." I know it's corny, but also so true. I was finally introduced to a wonderful doctor who is in the field of stem cells. I am so grateful I was able to speak with this gentleman and get his advice because he helped me find a facility in Germany.

During his research he discovered this facility in Lenggries, Germany, where they extract embryonic stem cells from sheep that live in the mountains, have limited contact with humans, and are protected by the government. Europe has the same views as the United States does on using human embryonic stem cells, but they are still open and progressive enough to find alternatives. This facility has been treating and curing people for over sixty years.

All the arrows were starting to point to Germany for my solution. I started corresponding with the doctor at the facility in September 2018. He was so patient with me and all my questions. He answered them all honestly, and was very forthcoming. Since schwannomatosis is so rare, the facility had never treated anyone like me before, and couldn't guarantee it would help my tumors. They were confident that my arthritis, asthma, stomach issues, and damaged nerves would heal, but for the tumors in my nerves, it was an experiment.

Even with all this research, I was still very apprehensive because this was such unknown territory for me. My doctors in the States could only advise me not to receive stem cell treatments in the US. Well, that wasn't very helpful except that it saved me from spending thousands of dollars on using my own stem cells because that was all that was being used at the time in the States —your own cells, which are not viable. They were extracting stem cells from the patient and then reinjecting them back into the patient. Once stem cells reach adulthood, they have reached their full potential. So if you inject your own stem cells back into you, it may help healthy people feel revitalized, but it does nothing for people like me.

Think of embryonic stem cells as building blocks. They develop organs, tissue, nerves, and bones. Young, fresh stem cells can help heal and rebuild tissues, organs, etc. Old stem cells are done growing and no longer will help heal damaged areas. Here are some examples from the German facility's website on what stem cells can help with:

- burnout syndrome
- after operations
- forgetfulness
- sleep disorders
- existential anxiety
- cardiovascular disease
- osteoporosis

- degenerative damage
- gastrointestinal disorders
- arthritis, and so much more.

Stem cell therapy is also used as an additional treatment after cancer. So needless to say, I went to Lenggries and received stem cell injections.

My husband and I traveled across the world for me to receive treatment, to potentially help improve my quality of life, which is a crazy thought in itself. It was a long and tiring journey, but so worth it. We were there for ten days, and I received over seventy-two different types of stem cells; all were injected eleven times into my butt with five-inch needles, which hurt like hell. After the injections, I had to lie on my stomach for almost an hour. Even afterwards, I couldn't walk; I had dead legs, and my hubby had to carry me to the bathroom. I am so grateful he was by my side; he's been such an incredible support system for me.

Seven weeks after the injections, there was a decrease in my pain flares. My pain that was in my stomach 24/7, accompanied by nausea, was completely gone; I was able to eat again. I had lost so much weight from not being able to eat due to the severe stomach pain. I basically lived off apple sauce for almost a year. I have a mass on one of my ovaries, and it used to cause excruciating pain; that pain has only flared up a few times since the stem cell treatment. My asthma is exponentially better; I've only used my inhaler a handful of times since, and I used to need it every day. To go out and do things with friends I used to need a wheelchair. Now I am walking and able to socialize.

My quality of life has improved drastically. I use to be bedridden or wrapped up in my heating pad on the couch, trying to remain positive and not give up on life. Now, I am able to go for walks with my family and enjoy the world around me again.

My goal in sharing my story is to help more people receive the treatment they need, and improve their quality of life. Being in chronic pain can feel very lonely, so don't stop looking for your solution. Even if it's not stem cells, there are countless alternative options in the world; you just have to find what's right for you. Don't stop searching.

Parting Advice

"There is nothing like you, there was nothing like you, and there shall be nothing like you." -Yogi tea bag tag

Let your beauty and uniqueness shine. No matter what your story may be or what battles you're fighting, we're all so individual and experience life so differently; your experience is just that: yours and yours alone. Make this life worth living. Make it worthwhile. The greatest gift you can give to another is your true, authentic self. Don't wait for permission from someone else to live your life. Don't wait for a disease or sickness to derail you before you see that you can live your life the way you want; you don't need anyone's permission to do so.

My disease gave me permission to live, permission I had been seeking from others but not myself. I didn't realize I was waiting for permission to live my life until my disease changed it drastically. The techniques discussed in this book have helped me become who I am today, able to live a beautiful life with pain.

Navigating a disease or any type of pain can be scary and feel very lonely. Please know that you are not alone in your struggles. Reach out to the people in your life, and tell them what you're going through and what you need from them. If I hadn't expressed any of this to my husband, I don't know if he would have been able to stick around and help. People want to help; they just don't know how or where to begin because there's no handbook to tell you, or them, how to deal with any of this.

Communication is huge in any type of relationship, but so particularly vital when going through something like chronic pain, or a disease. Don't bottle up what you're feeling. Talk it over and work it out with your loved ones. I know it's scary to be so open and vulnerable, but if you don't, you will continue to push people away and feel alone. Some days all I needed from my husband was to know that he loved me and that he was there with me because in all honesty, that's all he could do when I was in the depths of pain.

Having people in your corner who know what you are experiencing and going through is critical to your health and happiness. They can help advocate for you. There were times I felt so depleted and weak that if I hadn't had my husband to be an advocate for me, I would have been walked all over. Lean on your loved ones, and be open with them. They truly want to help; you've just got to guide them to what you need. Don't give up on yourself and trust in your strength.

Be patient. I didn't change overnight. It took time to develop a solid routine that helped not only my body but my mentality as well. When you're in the depths of depression, nothing I say will help, but it's okay if the only reason you got out of bed today was to take care of a pet or even a plant. Remember to find the little things in life that bring you joy and latch onto those like a rope being tossed out to you in the middle of the ocean while you're drowning.

Some days just a cup of tea helps me remember the good in life. Whatever it may be, don't judge yourself for it; tell that annoying voice to shut up. Stick with the routine. Your brain learns by repetition so it will automatically default to negativity if that's all its been taught. It takes time to create new pathways in the brain that become the default setting. Don't get discouraged if you don't see or feel results instantly, but don't give up either. You have the strength and the mental capacity to change and rewire your brain.

Lastly, getting a second opinion is always a good rule of thumb when it comes to surgeries or treatments. Some are willing to cut you open on a whim, and that's when you run into trouble. I learned this the hard way; for my first shoulder surgery I should have gotten a second opinion. It would have saved me unnecessary pain in the future. That doctor botched my torn ligament reattachment surgery and ended up causing me more issues in the long run that had to be fixed later on down the road. By getting a second opinion I found my amazing neurosurgeon at UW

Medical Center in Seattle! So always get a second opinion; learn from my mistake.

A Happy Ending ...

I can't say this is the ending, but rather the beginning of a new chapter in my life. It's been a little over two years since I decided to change my mentality, and I'm so glad I did. My life is such a blessing because of the choice to not let pain dictate how I live. Yes, I still have pain, but I now have an arsenal of tools to help me cope and work through it so I can live an abundant life with pain. It's been six months since my stem cell injections and I'm able to walk around and not be bed- or couch-ridden. I was able to go to a friend's wedding and dance, something I haven't been able to do in years. I'm excited I don't have to be excluded from life events anymore because of my pain. My quality of life has improved drastically.

We recently had to move back to Phoenix, Arizona, and I would not have been able to make this move without the stem cell treatment. I'm not the biggest fan of Phoenix because I spent most of my adolescent years trying to find a way out. So I've definitely been putting my living-in-the-present moment and gratitude practice to work. What is exciting about moving back to Arizona is that it gives us the opportunity to travel. I've been stuck in a house for three years in severe pain, and now I get the chance to travel again, something I thought would never happen. I feel like I got a second lease on life.

We've moved to a place that has a pool so I can add in different water exercises and strengthen my body in a different manner. I've found being in water helps alleviate pressure off of my tumors. My relationships with my family and friends are healthy and flourishing, unlike in the beginning where they had no idea how to deal with me, and I didn't know how to deal with any of this, which makes it difficult to have any type of relationship.

It feels so surreal sometimes to think that six months ago I needed a wheelchair to leave the house and now I am walking of my own accord. To go from being wheelchair bound to walking freely is a gift that is indescribable. I never thought my life would have turned out this way, but I am grateful for all the lessons along the way because now I can say I love this beautiful life, even with my pain.

The Buddhists have a saying, "*The lotus is a flower that grows in the mud. The thicker and deeper the mud, the more beautiful the lotus blooms.*" I love this saying because you can take your pain and struggles, and grow from them. Remember to find beauty in the pain.

Bibliography

Breuning, Loretta. "How to Train Your Brain to Go Positive Instead of Negative."
Forbes, 21
    Dec. 2016, www.forbes.com/sites/womensmedia/2016/12/21/how-to-
    train-your-brain-to-go-positive-instead-of-negative/#5e6ac5465a58.

Cedars-Sinai Medical Center. "Scientists recreate blood-brain barrier defect outside the body."
    ScienceDaily. ScienceDaily, 6 June 2019. <www.sciencedaily.com/re-
    leases/2019/06/190606133837.htm>

"Cord Blood Stem Cells: Current Uses and Future Challenges." *Eurostemcell.org,*
    www.eurostemcell.org/cord-blood-stem-cells-current-uses-and-future-
challenges.

Dolan, Eric W. "Meditation and Yoga Practice Linked to Reduced Volume in
Brain Region Tied
    to Negative Emotions." *PsyPost,* 18 Aug. 2019, www.psypost.org/2019/08/
    meditation-and-yoga-practice-linked-to-reduced-volume-in-brain-
    region-tied-to-negative-emotions-54273.

Gibson, Mel, and Neil Riordan. "Joe Rogan Experience #1066 – Mel Gibson & Dr.
Neil
    Riordan." *YouTube,* YouTube, 17 Jan. 2018, https://www.youtube.com/
    watch?v=OtL1fEEtLaA.

Hebrew University of Jerusalem. "First 'Haploid' Human Stem Cells Could
Change the Face of
    Medical Research." ScienceDaily, 28 June 2017. www.sciencedaily.com/
    releases/2017/06/170628131826.htm.

Hebrew University of Jerusalem. "Scientists Generate an Atlas of the Human
Genome Using
    Stem Cells: Human Gene Atlas Opens Up New Avenues for Studying
    Cancer and Genetic Disorders." ScienceDaily, 23 April 2018. www.sci-
    encedaily.com/releases/2018/04/180423155036.htm.

Izrael, M, et al. "Safety and Efficacy of Human Embryonic Stem Cell-derived
Astrocytes
    Following Intrathecal Transplantation in SOD1G93A and NSG Animal
    Models." *Stem Cell Research and Therapy*, vol. 9, no. 1, 6 June 2018, p. 152,

doi:10.1186/s13287-018-0890-5.

Korb, Alex. "The Grateful Brain." *Psychology Today*, 20 Nov. 2012,
     www.psychologytoday.com/us/blog/prefrontal-nudity/201211/the-grate-
ful-brain.

Lewandowski, W, et al. "Biological Mechanisms Related to the Effectiveness of
Guided Imagery
     for Chronic Pain." *Biological Research for Nursing*, vol. 13, no. 4, Oct. 2011,
     pp. 364-75, doi:10.1177/1099800410386475.

Onieva-Zafra, María Dolores, et al. "Effectiveness of Guided Imagery Relaxation
on Levels of
     Pain and Depression in Patients Diagnosed With Fibromyalgia." *Holis-
     tic Nursing Practice*, vol. 29, no. 1, Jan. 2015, pp. 13-21, doi: 10.1097/
     HNP.0000000000000062.

O, Goldstein, et al. "Mapping Whole-Transcriptome Splicing in Mouse
     Hematopoietic Stem Cells." *Stem Cell Reports*, vol. 8, no. 1, 10 Jan. 2017, pp.
     163-76, doi:10.1016/j.stemcr.2016.12.002.

Rahn, Bailey. "Cannabis's Entourage Effect: Why Whole Plant Medicine Matter-
s." *Leafly*, 28
     Oct. 2015, www.leafly.com/news/cannabis-101/cannabis-entourage-
     effect-why-thc-and-cbd-only-medicines-arent-g.

Rizvanov, Albert A et al. "Hematopoietic and Mesenchymal Stem Cells in Bio-
medical and
     Clinical Applications." *Stem Cells International* vol. 2016 (2016):
     3157365. doi:10.1155/2016/3157365

Ruiz, Don Miguel. *The Four Agreements: A Practical Guide to Personal Freedom.*
Amber-Allen
     Publishing, Inc, 1997.

Saingam, Darika, et al. "Pattern and Consequences of Krathom (Mitragyna spe-
ciosa Korth.) Use
     Among Male Villagers in Southern Thailand: A Qualitative Study." *In-
     ternational Journal of Drug Policy*, vol. 24, no. 4, July
     2013, pp. 351-58, doi:10.1016/j.drugpo.2012.09.004, www.news-med-
     ical.net/news/20190605/Chronic-inflammation-removes-motivation-by-
     reducing-dopamine-in-the-brain.aspx.

Schwartz, Allan. *Progress in Brain Research*, vol. 244, 14 Aug. 2009,
     www.mentalhelp.net/blogs/the-incredible-human-brain-
     neuroplasticity-and-the-power-of-positive-thinking/.

Schwartz, Allan. "The Incredible Human Brain, Neuroplasticity, and the Power
of Positive
     Thinking." *MentalHelp.net*, 14 Aug. 2009, www.mentalhelp.net/blogs/
     the-incredible-human-brain-neuroplasticity-and-the-power-of-positive-

thinking/.

Siegel-Itzkovich, Judy. "Breakthrough Offers Hope for Treatment of Lou Gehrig's Disease." *The*
Jerusalem Post, 23 May 2018, www.jpost.com/HEALTH-SCIENCE/ Breakthrough-offers-hope-for-treatment-of-Lou-Gehrigs-disease-558178.

Thomas, Liji. "Chronic Inflammation Removes Motivation by Reducing Dopamine in the
Brain." *News-medical.net*, 5 June 2019, www.news-medical.net/ news/20190605/Chronic-inflammation-removes-motivation-by-reducing-dopamine-in-the-brain.aspx.

Vukasin, Jovanovic M. et al. "BMP/SMAD Pathway Promotes Neurogenesis of Midbrain Dopaminergic Neurons In Vivo and in Human Induced Pluripotent and Neural Stem Cells." *The Journal of Neuroscience*, vol. 38, no. 7, 14 Feb. 2018, pp. 1662-76, doi:doi.org/10.1523/JNEUROSCI.1540-17.2018.

Additional websites I consulted in my research for this book:

https://drjoedispenza.com

https://en-med.tau.ac.il/stem_cells_regenerative

www.healthjourneys.com

www.mindvalley.com

This is the clinic in Panama I mentioned in the book. This link shows Dr. Neil Riordan's books as well:

https://www.cellmedicine.com/stem-cell-therapy/video-stem-cell-therapy/ stem-cell-lectures/neil-riordan-phd/

CPSIA information can be obtained
at www.ICGtesting.com
Printed in the USA
LVHW110746111119
636960LV00011B/4726/P